HE

Library+

AIDS

Jo Whelan

Wayland

an imp... ...en's Books

© 2002 White-Thomson Publishing Ltd

White-Thomson Publishing Ltd,
2-3 St Andrew's Place,
Lewes, East Sussex BN7 1UP

Published in Great Britain in 2002 by Hodder Wayland, an imprint of Hodder Children's Books

Reprinted in 2002

This paperback edition published in 2003.

This book was produced for White-Thomson Publishing Ltd by Ruth Nason.

Design: Carole Binding
Picture research: Glass Onion Pictures

The right of Jo Whelan to be identified as the author of this work has been asserted by her in accordance with the Copyright, Designs and Patents Act 1988.

British Library Cataloguing in Publication Data
Whelan, Jo
    AIDS. - (Health Issues)
    1. AIDS (Disease)
    I. Title
    616.9'792

ISBN 0 7502 3542 X

Printed in Italy by G. Canale & C.S.p.A.

Hodder Children's Books
A division of Hodder Headline Limited
338 Euston Road, London NW1 3BH

Acknowledgements

The author and publishers thank the following for their permission to reproduce photographs and illustrations: Camera Press: cover and page 1; Martyn Chillmaid: page 4; Corbis Images: pages 14 (Jeremy Horner), 24 (Roger Ressmeyer), 28 (Peter Turnley), 31 (Jacques M. Chenet), 33, 34 (Wolfgang Kaehler), 36 (Jennie Woodcock), 38 (Steve Raymer), 42 (Annie Griffiths Belt), 50 (Roger Ressmeyer); GAZE: page 15; Angela Hampton Family Life Pictures: page 37; Robert Harding Picture Library: page 23; Impact: pages 7, 35, 47, 48; Pictorial Press: page 55; Popperfoto: pages 8, 12, 13, 16, 27, 30, 41, 59; Science Photo Library: pages 6, 9, 18, 20, 21, 22, 25, 26, 29, 43, 44, 49, 54; Tony Stone Images: pages 56, 58; Topham Picturepoint: pages 11, 10, 17, 53; Wayland Picture Library: pages 19, 57.

Contents

Introduction
The virus and the disease

'The potential for mass destruction of such large sections of humanity has never been so great as is the case with this disease.'
(Professor Barry D. Schoub, an internationally respected AIDS specialist)

Until 1982, no one had heard of AIDS. Since then it has become one of the most feared diseases in history and has killed over 15 million people, most of them young or middle-aged. Millions more are infected with HIV – the virus that causes AIDS – so the death toll will keep on rising. Because people with HIV are infectious to others for the rest of their lives, the number of infected people is growing all the time. At the moment, the risk of catching AIDS is relatively small for most groups of people living in the Western or developed world. However, thousands of new infections take place every year, so no one can afford to be complacent. Knowing the facts can help you protect yourself.

AIDS stands for Acquired Immunodeficiency Syndrome, which is the end result of infection with the Human Immunodeficiency Virus, or HIV. The virus gradually destroys the immune system until it can no longer fight off infections. People with AIDS suffer from repeated infections, often from bacteria and viruses that are harmless to healthy people. They become progressively weaker until eventually one of the infections kills them.

AIDS ribbons
Red ribbons are worn to show solidarity in the fight against AIDS.

The AIDS memorial quilt
Each panel of this quilt is a memorial to someone who died of AIDS. Over 44,000 panels have been made so far. They are exhibited around the world to raise awareness about AIDS. Here the whole quilt is seen in Washington DC in the USA.

AIDS is unique in the reactions it causes. It arouses great fear because it leads to suffering and death, and there is so far no cure. The fact that it is spread mainly through sex means that it is also seen as something shameful. People are embarrassed to talk about it, and those infected often face prejudice and hostility.

In this book, we begin by looking at the scale of the AIDS epidemic around the world (chapter 1). Chapter 2 looks at how our immune systems work and how HIV attacks them, and chapter 3 describes the symptoms and effects of AIDS itself. Chapter 4 describes how the virus is spread, and chapter 5 discusses ways to avoid infection. Chapter 6 deals with HIV tests and looks at the treatments available. Finally, chapter 7 explores society's reactions to AIDS and the experiences of people living with the virus. Definitions of some of the more specialized terms used in the book can be found in the glossary on page 60. The resources section on page 62 gives details of where to find information and support.

1 The AIDS epidemic
Its effects around the world

The emergence of AIDS

In late 1980 and early 1981, doctors in Los Angeles, California, reported that five previously healthy young men had become seriously ill with a rare type of pneumonia caused by a fungus called *Pneumocystis carinii*. This had only been seen before in people whose immune systems were severely damaged by medical drugs or certain diseases. All of the five were gay (homosexual) and sexually active. In 1981 came reports of 26 gay men in New York and California with a rare cancer called Kaposi's sarcoma. Most of the men in these reports also had other infections that are usually restricted to people with damaged immune systems.

Throughout 1981 reports of such unusual infections continued to rise, almost all in sexually active gay men from cities with large gay communities, and a few in people who injected illegal drugs like heroin. There were also many cases in the same groups of people of persistently swollen glands and unexplained flu-like symptoms. Doctors and public health authorities began to realize that something new was happening that involved a weakening of the immune system, but did not know what could be causing it. In 1982 they named the mystery condition Acquired Immunodeficiency Syndrome,

The USA
A doctor examines a man with AIDS in San Francisco, California.

shortened to AIDS, and drew up a set of medical signs and symptoms to define it.

In 1982 the US media picked up the story, with reports of a 'gay cancer' (Kaposi's sarcoma). People began to fear that any contact with gay men – a group already facing prejudice – might pass on the mystery disease. Gay men were also fearful as more of them started to get ill and die.

Other developed countries were also looking for and finding AIDS. Then in 1983 doctors in France and Belgium noticed that AIDS patients who came from Africa did not fall into the same groups as the others: around half were women, most of the men were heterosexual and most were not drug injectors. Investigators began looking in these patients' home countries and discovered that AIDS was spreading through Africa as well, mainly via heterosexual sex (sex between men and women).

Tanzania

A doctor talks with an AIDS patient in Tanzania.

The search for the AIDS virus

At first, no one knew what was causing AIDS. Theories included drug abuse and an overload of sexually transmitted infections (STIs), both of which were common in the large, active gay communities that were suffering most from the disease. But it gradually became clear that the link between the illnesses was some kind of infection that was being spread by sex and was causing people's immune systems to collapse. Then in late 1982 doctors realized that AIDS was also spreading through blood transfusions and products made from blood. These included the products used to treat haemophilia, a genetic condition that stops blood clotting properly.

In 1983, a team of scientists at the Pasteur Institute in Paris, led by Luc Montagnier, discovered a substance called reverse transcriptase in cells taken from someone with AIDS. Reverse transcriptase is an enzyme made only by a family of viruses called the retroviruses (see page 22). Using an electron microscope, the scientists saw a new virus which they called LAV. In 1984 they showed that LAV kills T-helper cells, the part of the immune system that is

Researchers

Luc Montagnier (left), Myron Essex (centre) and Robert C. Gallo won medical research awards in 1986 for their work on AIDS.

damaged in AIDS. Meanwhile, Robert Gallo's group at the National Institutes of Health in the USA was working in the same area, and in 1983 they also linked AIDS to a retrovirus. At first Gallo's team thought it was HTLV-1, a virus already known to cause leukaemia. Then in 1984 they succeeded in growing the virus – now renamed HTLV-III – in their laboratory.

It turned out that both teams had discovered the virus that causes AIDS. But who got there first? A big argument arose over who should get the credit, not least because the winning institution would make huge amounts of money from selling tests for the virus. The dispute was eventually settled at a meeting between President Reagan of the USA and President Mitterand of France, who agreed that credit would be shared and money from test sales would go to a fund for AIDS research in the developing world. An international committee gave the virus its permanent name: Human Immunodeficiency Virus, or HIV for short.

HIV
This coloured electron micrograph shows Human Immunodeficiency Viruses (HIV) emerging from a white blood cell. The viruses are shown in green.

Once the virus was identified, research took off. Scientists now know more about HIV than probably any other micro-organism, and there are signs that this knowledge might at last be bearing fruit in the form of effective treatment (see chapter 6).

Where did HIV come from?

Scientists are fairly sure that HIV is a new virus, at least for humans. The first evidence of it is in a frozen blood sample taken from a man in the Democratic Republic of the Congo in 1959. However, similar viruses infect African monkeys and chimpanzees, and most researchers now think that humans became infected from chimpanzees when they killed the animals for food. Another theory blames the early polio vaccines, which were prepared using monkey tissue and tried out in Africa in the 1950s. However, the most recent research shows that vaccines are very unlikely to have introduced the virus.

Wherever it originated, we know from stored blood samples that HIV was very uncommon anywhere before the late 1970s, and that the epidemic appeared almost at the same time in the USA, Europe and Africa. The factors that allowed it to spread include more frequent international travel, an increase in drug abuse by injecting, the worldwide trade in donated blood products and the rise in sexual activity outside marriage.

Drug injecting
One way in which HIV spreads is when drug users share needles.

The AIDS epidemic

The United Nations estimates that about 47 million people around the world had been infected with HIV by the end of 1998. Of these, about 14 million have died and 33 million are living with the virus. Because AIDS often takes years to develop (see chapter 3), many people do not know they are infected. Almost 6 million people catch HIV each year – that's about 16,000 each day. Worldwide, AIDS is the fourth most common cause of death in adults. Countries are affected in different ways, and the biggest difference is between those of the rich, developed world and those of the poorer, developing world, especially Africa.

Aids in the developing world

About 95 per cent of people with HIV live in the developing world, and 70 per cent in Africa south of the Sahara Desert, which is known as sub-Saharan Africa. Up to the end of 1998 AIDS had killed 11.5 million people in this region – 83 per cent of all AIDS deaths so far. A quarter of those killed have been children, most of them infected by their mothers as babies. Because of the numbers of people already infected with HIV, the death rate will carry on rising for many years. In the worst-affected countries, more than 1 in 5 people between the ages of 15 and 49 carry the virus. Many other African countries have infection rates of 1 in 10 or higher.

Throughout the developing world, sex between men and women (heterosexual sex) is by far the commonest way for the virus to spread. The danger starts young, especially for girls. One study in part of Kenya found that 1 in 5 girls aged 15-19 was infected. Most had caught HIV from sex with older men. Overall, in the developing world, about half of people who get the virus pick it up before they are 25. Most of these die from AIDS before their 35th birthday.

Infected at birth
A 10 month-old baby infected with AIDS in Cape Town, South Africa.

An AIDS hospice
Hospices provide care for people who are dying and also give emotional support to their families.

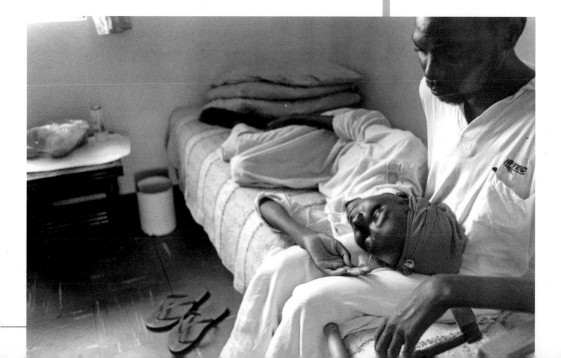

AIDS orphans

Many people who die of AIDS in Africa leave children behind. By the end of 1999, around 11 million children under 15 had lost their mothers from AIDS, with many losing fathers as well. Millions of others have been plunged into desperate poverty because their parents are too ill to work or look after them. Often these children have to leave school to earn money, help with the crops or care for their parents. Some end up living on the streets. Those who become orphans must be cared for by relatives, putting added strain on already poor families. In Zambia, it is estimated that three-quarters of all families are caring for at least one AIDS orphan.

South Africa

US Surgeon General David Satcher (centre) poses with children orphaned by AIDS, during a visit to South Africa for an international AIDS conference.

Poverty is a major factor behind the spread of AIDS:

- Education about AIDS prevention has been held back by lack of money, and sometimes by unwillingness to talk about sex or use condoms.
- Good-quality condoms are often not available or too expensive.
- Lack of affordable healthcare means that other sexually transmitted infections go untreated. Having another STI makes it easier to catch HIV, because the virus can enter through sores or other areas of damaged skin.
- Poverty causes social problems. For example, men may have to work far away from their families. In this situation they often turn to prostitutes, many of whom carry HIV. For some women, selling sex is the only way to survive.

AIDS is having a devastating effect in countries already facing huge problems. Most of those who are ill or have died are, or were, young or middle-aged – the backbone of the workforce. In some areas this is causing shortages of workers, farmers and skilled professionals like doctors and nurses.

AIDS hits teachers and nurses in Kenya

Education in Kenya is under threat because at least 10,000 teachers there have died of AIDS in the last five years. The warning comes from Dr Sobbie Mulindi of the Kenya Institute of Education. He also says that AIDS will probably cause a drop in the number of children who complete their schooling.

Looking ahead, Dr Mulindi is pessimistic. He points out that 70-80 per cent of those infected with HIV in Kenya are young people, 'something that spells doom for the country'.

Meanwhile, hospitals in the Nyanza region are facing severe staff shortages, because more than 10 per cent of all nurses there are ill with AIDS.

'Every weekend we raise funds for staff funerals,' says Dr Ambrose Misore, the Provincial Medical Officer. Some hospital patients have to be looked after by relatives because there are not enough nurses to do the work. (Stories from 'The Nation' newspaper, Nairobi)

An AIDS vaccine?
Scientists in Kenya are among many working to develop a vaccine against AIDS.

In Asia and Latin America the epidemic was slower to start, but HIV infection is now rising fast in many countries. India, with its population of 1,000 million, has more people with HIV than any other single country.

A Thai family
The father of this family in Thailand has AIDS. His wife and children are HIV-positive.

AIDS in the developed world

Anyone who is sexually active can get HIV (unless neither partner has ever injected drugs or had sex with anyone else). But in the developed world, the risk of infection is higher for the following groups:

- men who have sex with men (both gay and bisexual)
- people who inject drugs
- people who have been sexually active in countries where HIV is common, especially south, east and central Africa
- sexual partners of any of the above.

Gay and bisexual men were the first to be affected by AIDS in the developed world and still make up the largest HIV-infected group. Infection rates are also high in injecting (intravenous) drug users, who account for the majority of cases in some cities.

So far, the virus is rare in the rest of the population. But heterosexual spread is rising, and is now the fastest-growing method of HIV infection. For example, in 1999 the UK saw more people catch HIV heterosexually than

A gay disease?

In the early days of the epidemic, AIDS was dubbed by the media as 'the gay plague'. Many people still wrongly believe that only homosexual men are at risk. In fact, sex between men and women accounts for 80-90 per cent of the world's HIV infections, and is the fastest-growing means of spread in the developed world.

No one knows how HIV got into the gay community, but once there its spread was made easier by the fact that some gay men have many different sexual partners. Also, anal sex carries a greater risk of infection because the delicate lining of the rectum is easily damaged, allowing the virus to enter the body. When gay men realized the danger from HIV, more of them started using condoms or switched to safer types of sex, and the spread of the epidemic slowed down. However, in the mid-1990s infection rates in gay men started rising again as some forgot the safer sex message.

Sexual partners
Anyone who is sexually active can be infected with HIV.

AIDS.
PREVENTION IS THE ONLY CURE WE'VE GOT

The grim reaper
Publicizing AIDS as a frightening killer disease was one way of persuading people to protect themselves in their sexual relationships.

homosexually – the first time this had happened. Many of these 1,340 heterosexual infections were probably picked up elsewhere in the world or through sex with bisexual men or drug injectors. But as these 'high-risk' groups infect their partners, who in turn have sex with people outside those groups, the virus will gradually spread into the wider population. How widespread it becomes will depend on people's sexual behaviour. When AIDS first came on the scene there were fears of a huge epidemic; some people predicted that by the year 2000, everyone would know someone who had the disease. This has not happened, but as the situation in Africa shows, it is not impossible. It is important for everyone to protect themselves from HIV and other sexually transmitted infections – ways of doing this are discussed in chapter 5.

Some statistics

The UK

- About 30,000 people are living with HIV; a third of them do not realize they are infected.
- Around 12,000 people have died of AIDS.
- Over 2,500 new HIV infections are diagnosed each year.

The USA

- 733,000 cases of AIDS since the epidemic began.
- 425,000 have died.
- Up to 900,000 people are living with HIV.
- 2,000 new AIDS cases in the 13-24 age group in 1998.

In the early 1980s, thousands of people caught HIV through blood transfusions and blood products. People with the blood disease haemophilia were badly affected because the products they need are extracted from blood pooled together from hundreds of donors. However, since the mid-1980s all donated blood in the developed world has been screened (tested) to make sure it is free from infection, and the risk from transfusions is now extremely small. Having a blood transfusion in other parts of the world is risky.

Blood transfusion

Transfusions can spread HIV, so all donated blood must be screened.

2 The immune system and HIV

Under attack

Every day, our bodies come under attack from invisible enemies in the form of bacteria, viruses, fungi and microscopic animals (conveniently lumped together under the term 'microbes'). Our skin, mouth and intestines are home to billions of bacteria, most of them harmless but some potentially dangerous if they are not kept in check. The immune system is the body's way of dealing with these microbes to stop them from harming us. In people with AIDS the system has been partially destroyed by the HIV virus and no longer works properly, so they are unable to fight off infection in the normal way.

Devouring an invader

In this hugely magnified coloured electron micrograph, a type of white blood cell called a macrophage has stretched out to capture an invading microbe (pink).

The immune system

The immune system is a complex and fascinating network of cells and messenger chemicals which protect us from infection and disease. Scientists are still finding out how it all works, and much of this research is driven by the search for a cure or vaccine for AIDS. Here we will describe it in a very simplified way.

The first line of defence is the skin. Healthy, unbroken skin is an effective barrier against most microbes. Those that do get into the body usually enter through the openings at the mouth or genitals, the lungs, or through cuts or sores. Once inside they come into contact with various specialized cell types which are programmed to recognize and destroy invaders. Some of these specialized cells live in the tissues and some in the blood, where they are known as white blood cells.

Some white blood cells and their tissue-dwelling cousins kill invaders by swallowing them up or by releasing special toxins (poisons). They then present protein particles – a sort of chemical signature – from their prey to other white cells called lymphocytes. The lymphocytes produce tailor-made proteins called antibodies which stick to the signature protein whenever they come across it on an invader or on the surface of an infected cell. The antibodies act as a signal to the first set of white cells, which move in for the kill as already described. The lymphocytes also 'remember' the signature, and if that microbe enters the body again they make antibodies to get rid of it straight away. This is why many illnesses only affect us once; after that, we are immune to them.

If a microbe multiplies enough before the immune system can stop it, we become ill. But in most cases the system

Illness
When a microbe overcomes our immune system, we become ill – but the system normally fights back.

T-helper (CD4) cells: victims of the killer virus

One type of white cell – the T-lymphocyte – makes chemicals similar to antibodies, but instead of releasing them into the blood it keeps them on its surface. When it comes across the relevant signature protein it sticks to the offending microbe or cell and either kills it (T-killer cells) or sends out chemical messengers which help other lymphocytes to do their job. These T-helper cells, also known as CD4 cells, play a vital co-ordinating role. Without them, the immune system is severely damaged. Unfortunately, they are also the main target of the HIV virus, which invades and kills them (see page 23).

catches up within a few days, wiping out the microbes and allowing us to recover. If the immune system is swamped and loses control, infections can take hold and eventually kill.

Microbes that cause disease

Many of the illnesses and diseases we experience are caused by bacteria or viruses. Both come in many different types, only a few of which are capable of infecting humans. Bacteria consist of a single cell, complete with everything it needs to live and reproduce. They can be killed by antibiotic drugs, though some have adapted to become resistant to them. Examples of diseases caused by bacteria include most stomach bugs, many coughs and sore throats, the most serious forms of meningitis and pneumonia, and sexually transmitted infections like gonorrhoea and chlamydia.

Viruses are very simple organisms consisting of nothing but some strands of genetic material (DNA or RNA), a protein coat and sometimes an outer envelope of proteins and fats. They cannot reproduce on their own but rely on using equipment hijacked from the cells of their host (the animal or plant they have infected). It is very difficult to kill them without damaging the host cell as well, so there are few anti-viral drugs available. Antibiotics don't work against viruses. Diseases caused by viruses include colds, flu, measles, herpes, and of course AIDS.

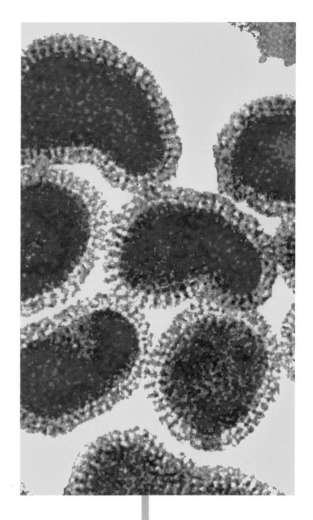

Flu viruses

An electron micrograph of a section through some flu viruses, showing a core of RNA (red) and a spiked protein envelope (green). The outer proteins allow the virus to enter cells when it invades the body.

We usually associate fungi with moulds or mushrooms, but some types can infect the body. Athlete's foot is a fungal infection, and thrush is caused by a type of fungus called a yeast. In people with damaged immune systems, fungi that are normally harmless can grow in the lungs and elsewhere. One disease caused in this way is *Pneumocystis carinii* pneumonia (PCP), which is common in people with AIDS.

The final category of disease-causing microbes is protozoa, which are tiny single-celled animals. The protozoa that infect humans (and other animals) live as parasites – that is, they rely on their host's body for food and shelter. Protozoal diseases include malaria and toxoplasmosis, a normally harmless infection which can damage the brain and other organs in AIDS.

The HIV virus

Despite its terrible effects, HIV is an average-sized and rather fragile virus. It has an outer envelope of proteins and fats that is easily damaged by heating or drying and by chemicals like detergents and disinfectants. Unlike some other viruses, it cannot survive outside the moist environment of the body fluids where it lives. This means it cannot be caught from toilet seats, door handles or other everyday items. Its outer envelope is covered in knobs

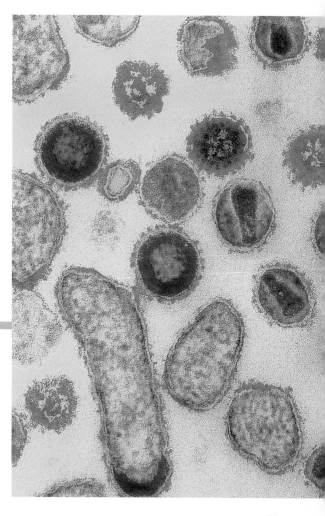

HIV viruses
A section through HIV viruses. An outer envelope (yellow), spiked with proteins, surrounds a conical protein core (red). The core shields the genetic material, RNA.

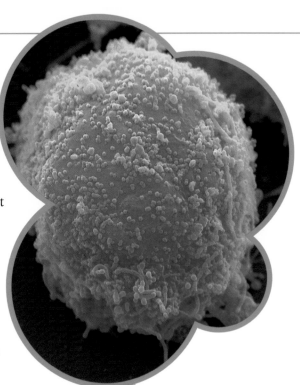

made from a protein known as gp120, which acts like a key to enable the virus to enter the immune system's CD4 (T-helper) cells.

Inside the envelope is the protein coat or capsid, which is conical in shape. Within this lies the genetic material – two strands of RNA. Because it contains RNA not DNA, HIV is classified in a group known as retroviruses. To reproduce, the virus uses the genetic machinery inside CD4 cells to make copies of itself, which

Hijacking the cell

Retroviruses like HIV have a unique ability to become a permanent part of the cells they infect. Once inside the cell the virus uses an enzyme called reverse transcriptase to convert its own genetic material (RNA) into DNA, the molecule that carries the human genetic code. The DNA copy of the viral genes then inserts itself into one of the cell's chromosomes, becoming part of the set of instructions that direct the cell's behaviour. When the DNA activates it hijacks the host cell, directing it to make thousands of copies of HIV RNA and assemble them into new viruses. The cell itself is weakened and dies.

When the cell divides, the viral DNA is passed on to the new cells created. The only way to get rid of the virus would be to kill every single one of the infected cells – without killing the patient! It may never be possible to find a way of doing this.

An infected cell
A T-lymphocyte white blood cell (orange in this electron micrograph) has been infected with HIV viruses (blue). The viruses are budding away from the cell membrane. They will enter the bloodstream and infect more T-lymphocytes.

then break out of the cell and circulate in the blood, semen (sperm fluid), vaginal fluids and breast milk. From there they go on to infect more CD4 cells – and, if the opportunity arises, move into a new host person.

Destroying the immune system

When HIV enters the body it begins reproducing immediately, building up huge numbers of new virus particles in the blood and infecting and killing millions of CD4 cells. The immune system makes a brave effort to get rid of it. Killer lymphocytes recognize and destroy infected CD4 cells. Antibodies are created, and within a few weeks the number of viruses in the blood falls sharply and the number of CD4 cells rises again. A sort of balance is achieved: HIV is still multiplying and killing CD4 cells, but antibodies and killer cells are keeping virus numbers in check and the dead cells are being replaced.

Gradually, HIV gains the upper hand. Over a period of years the number of CD4 cells gets less and the immune system becomes less efficient. In the end, it can no longer provide a proper defence, and the person begins to suffer from the collection of infections that are typical of AIDS. The infections are long-lasting and severe because the body has lost its ability to fight them off. At the same time HIV is able to multiply more freely, and the immune system deteriorates further. Eventually the person dies, usually from an infection.

Deterioration
A person with AIDS becomes progressively weaker as their immune system fails.

Nu... ...t 4A

Nursin... ...t 4B

→ Nurs... ...Unit 4C

3 AIDS: the disease
Its symptoms and effects

AIDS is the final stage of HIV infection. Most of the symptoms of AIDS are not caused by the HIV virus itself but by other infections which get past the damaged immune system. Doctors have drawn up a list of 25 infections and conditions that are known as AIDS-defining: any HIV-infected person who gets one of these is classed as having AIDS. The health of the immune system can be judged by counting the number of CD4 cells (see page 19) per cubic millimetre (mm^3) of blood. HIV-infected people are also classed as having AIDS when the CD4 count falls below a certain level, whether or not they have had an AIDS-defining infection.

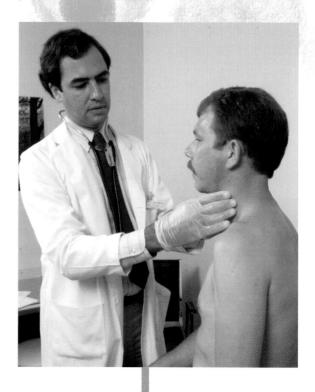

Monitoring
A doctor monitors the health of a patient infected with HIV.

First signs of infection

When first infected with the HIV virus, about 50 per cent of people get flu-like symptoms such as swollen glands, fever, aches and pains and tiredness. They may also lose their appetite and have sickness and diarrhoea. These symptoms can last anything from a few days to a few weeks, and some people feel tired or depressed for a while afterwards. Most people think they have had flu or some other virus, and do not realize they have caught HIV. The other 50 per cent experience no symptoms at all. During this period the virus is multiplying freely; there are huge numbers of virus particles in the blood, semen and vaginal fluids, so the person is very infectious.

The silent period

After any initial symptoms have died down, the infected person feels fit and well again. Their health stays normal for anything from 1 to 15 years, 10 years being the average in the developed world. The disease usually develops more quickly in countries where healthcare is poor. As explained in chapter 2, HIV is active during the silent period but is kept partially under control by the immune system. Nevertheless, the number of CD4 cells slowly falls as they are killed faster than they can be replaced. Since the late 1990s, drugs have been available which can make the silent period last much longer by stopping the virus from multiplying (see chapter 6).

About 5 per cent of people show little fall in their CD4 counts for 10-15 years or even longer; scientists are very interested in finding out why this group is able to resist the virus so well, as it may hold clues to possible treatments.

HIV can still be passed on during the silent period.

Resistance

Women working as prostitutes in Kenya are at high risk of infection with HIV, but some seem to be resistant to it. Their blood is being studied to find out more.

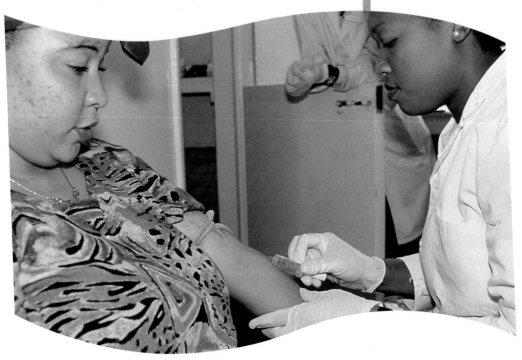

Early HIV disease

A normal CD4 count is 500-1200 cells per mm^3. When the count falls below 500, the first symptoms usually begin to show. These include:

- skin rashes
- flu-like symptoms
- persistent swollen glands
- recurring diarrhoea
- weight loss.

The person may also begin to suffer from infections like thrush (a yeast infection of the mouth or vagina), shingles (a painful rash that appears in bands on the upper body), and oral hairy leukoplakia (a particular type of abnormal white patches in the mouth, found only in people with HIV).

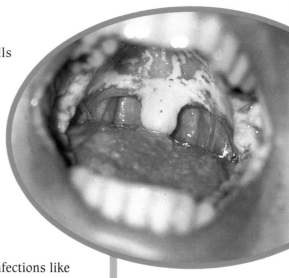

Oral thrush

A severe thrush infection (white patches) in an AIDS patient's mouth.

Advanced AIDS

When the CD4 count falls below 200, the person is classed as having AIDS. By now HIV has won its battle with the immune system and is multiplying rapidly. The person is at high risk of developing the range of infections, cancers and other problems that are characteristic of the disease – the AIDS-defining conditions. Some of the commonest are described on the following pages.

Many people with AIDS lose weight and gradually get weaker until they are no longer able to work or look after themselves. The severe weight loss is called wasting, and its exact cause is not known. Others have bouts of serious infection but recover quite well in between.

Opportunistic infections

Most of the infections that strike people with AIDS are called opportunistic. This means that they do not usually infect humans but will do so when the opportunity arises – normally when the immune system is weak. The bacteria, viruses, fungi and parasites that cause them are all around us, but are harmless to people with healthy immune systems.

Someone with advanced AIDS will usually die within 18 months to two years, though the latest drugs can improve this outlook. Death is usually caused by an opportunistic infection or cancer, or can be due to the effects of severe wasting.

Common infections and symptoms

Most people with AIDS suffer from at least one of the following infections. Often they will have more than one at a time, or several over a short period. The infections and symptoms are usually more severe and longer-lasting than in people with normal immune systems, and the person can become very ill. Pneumonia, tuberculosis and fungal infections can kill.

- severe and persistent diarrhoea, caused by various opportunistic bacteria and viruses
- pneumonia (severe lung infection), often caused by the fungus *Pneumocystis carinii*

Wasting

AIDS has had a wasting effect on the body of this young man at a hospice in Phnom Penh, Cambodia.

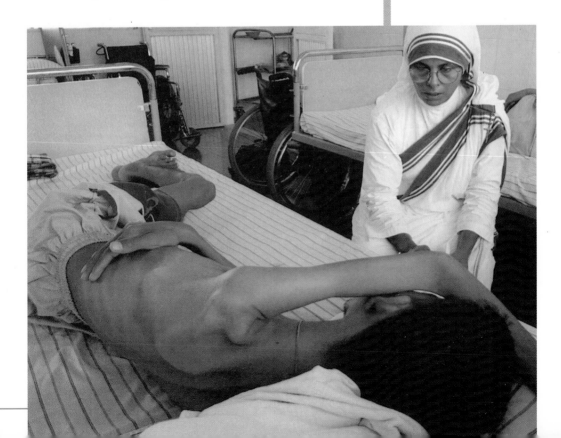

- visual problems and blindness, caused by a normally harmless virus called cytomegalovirus
- tuberculosis: this once-common lung disease has made a comeback in people with AIDS
- shingles
- sores and ulcers around the mouth and genitals, caused by the herpes virus
- fungal infections, sometimes spreading throughout the body

'At times I've felt so ill that I wanted to die. The hospital staff are fantastic though, and the support from them and from family and friends has kept me going through the really bad days.' (Sheila)

John

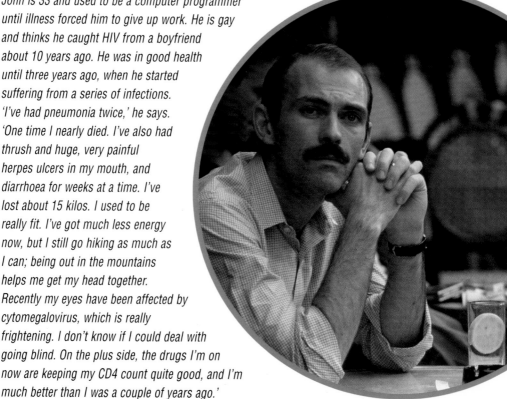

John is 33 and used to be a computer programmer until illness forced him to give up work. He is gay and thinks he caught HIV from a boyfriend about 10 years ago. He was in good health until three years ago, when he started suffering from a series of infections. 'I've had pneumonia twice,' he says. 'One time I nearly died. I've also had thrush and huge, very painful herpes ulcers in my mouth, and diarrhoea for weeks at a time. I've lost about 15 kilos. I used to be really fit. I've got much less energy now, but I still go hiking as much as I can; being out in the mountains helps me get my head together. Recently my eyes have been affected by cytomegalovirus, which is really frightening. I don't know if I could deal with going blind. On the plus side, the drugs I'm on now are keeping my CD4 count quite good, and I'm much better than I was a couple of years ago.'

Thelma

Thelma, 26, is South African and lives in a poor district on the edge of a large city. Home is a two-room shack made of corrugated iron. Thelma's husband died of AIDS last year. He was a miner and spent many months of the year away from home, and she knows he sometimes visited the prostitutes who make a living around the mining hostels. Now she is sick herself, with tuberculosis (TB). She has a severe cough, sometimes bringing up blood, and what seems like a constant fever. Her appetite has gone and she has lost so much weight that it is difficult to recognize her as the healthy, lively young woman that her friends knew before. She is now too weak to look after her children, so her eight year-old daughter misses school and takes care of the family with the help of an aunt who lives nearby. The doctor thinks Thelma's TB and weight loss are signs of AIDS, though she hasn't been tested. Even if she had, she could not afford the drugs that might slow the disease down. Thelma probably has just a few months to live.

AIDS and cancer

Certain cancers often affect people with AIDS. The best-known is Kaposi's sarcoma, a cancer of the blood vessels that is very rare in the rest of the population. It causes pink, purple or brown patches on the skin, and can also affect the internal organs. It can be fatal. Gay men are much more likely to get Kaposi's sarcoma than other groups of AIDS patients, so scientists think a sexually transmitted virus may be involved.

Kaposi's sarcoma

This cancer, causing dark skin lesions, is common in people with AIDS.

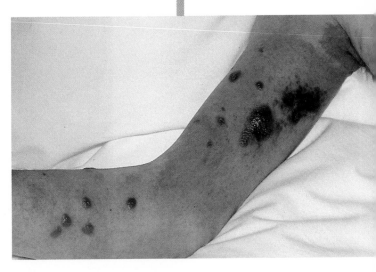

Women with AIDS have high rates of cervical cancer, which is caused by some types of sexually transmitted human papilloma virus.

Both sexes are affected by cancers of the lymphatic system, the network of fluid-filled channels that play a part in the immune system and which we feel as lymph glands in the neck and groin areas. These lymph cancers, known as lymphomas, often spread to other parts of the body. Symptoms include fever, sweating and weight loss. Again, it is suspected that a virus may be the cause.

AIDS and the nervous system

Up to half of people with advanced AIDS experience symptoms of the nervous system. Various opportunistic infections can affect the brain, causing headaches, meningitis (inflammation of the membranes around the brain), confusion, memory loss, lack of coordination and personality changes. The HIV virus itself lives in the brain and nervous system and probably causes direct damage. In severe cases it causes dementia, which is a serious loss of memory and other mental powers. It can also damage nerves around the body, leading to pain and numbness in the arms and legs.

People with AIDS often suffer from anxiety and depression. While this can have physical causes linked to nervous system damage, it is also an understandable reaction to the suffering and problems they face.

Double tragedy
Photographed in 1998, this five year-old boy was living in an orphanage for children with AIDS in Nairobi, Kenya.

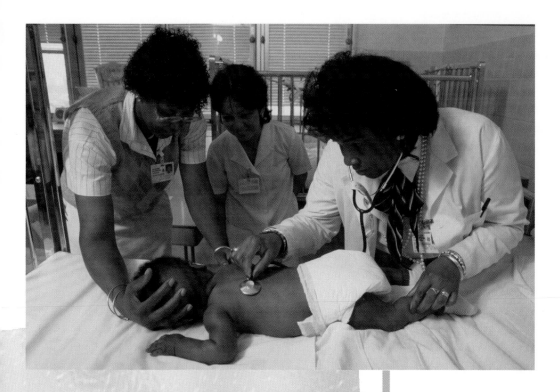

Children with AIDS

Around the world, about 1.2 million children are living with HIV or AIDS. Most caught the virus from their mothers as babies, and some got it from blood transfusions or blood products. Also affected are children (both boys and girls) who work as prostitutes, and girls who are married or made to have sex at a young age. Over 90 per cent of infected children live in the developing world. As well as facing ill-health themselves, most are likely to lose their mothers and perhaps their fathers to AIDS.

About 10-15 per cent of HIV-infected babies develop AIDS by the time they are three and die before they are five. Of the rest, many survive into their teens. Some suffer from repeated infections, though not necessarily the same ones that affect adults with AIDS. Others stay healthy for many years. In the developed world, many who would have died as children are now surviving into the teenage years, thanks to the new anti-viral drugs.

New York

Hospital staff looking after children with AIDS in Harlem, New York, have the benefit of modern facilities and equipment.

4 How HIV is spread
Are you at risk?

The HIV virus is present in the blood, semen (sperm fluid), male 'pre-come' fluid, vaginal fluids and breast milk of infected people. These contain both free viruses and infected cells. HIV can be passed on when any of these fluids enters the body of an uninfected person. There are three ways that this can happen:

- through sexual contact
- through contact with infected blood
- from a mother to her baby before or during birth or while breastfeeding.

Other body fluids – saliva, tears, urine and sweat – contain little or no virus and are therefore not infectious. The only possible exception is saliva, which may contain traces of blood. This means there is a very small risk that deep (French or tongue-in) kissing could spread HIV.

The virus has to have an easy entry point – it cannot get through unbroken skin but does pass through the moist linings of the vagina, penis, rectum (inside the anus), mouth and eyes. It can also get in through cuts and sores.

Sexual contact

Sexual contact accounts for about 90 per cent of all HIV infections worldwide, with sex between men and women by far the most common method of spread (although until recently, sex between men was the main cause of infection in the developed world). The virus can be passed on through vaginal sex (the penis entering the vagina), anal sex (the penis entering the anus) or oral sex (using the mouth to stimulate your partner's genitals). Masturbation (stimulating your partner's genitals with your hands) is unlikely to cause infection, although there would be a small risk if sexual fluids got in to broken skin.

What's the risk?

Having sex with an infected person does not automatically mean that you will catch HIV. In fact, HIV is a lot harder to catch than some other viruses. The risk of getting it is increased by two important factors:

- the stage of infection: people who have recently been infected and those with advanced AIDS have very high levels of virus in their body fluids, and are much more infectious than people in the 'silent' phase. Someone recently infected is unlikely to know about it, so their partners won't either.

- other infections: having another sexually transmitted infection – such as herpes, gonorrhoea or chlamydia – increases the risk of getting HIV. This is because the sores or inflammation caused by the other STI make it easier for the HIV virus to get in. Equally, the other STIs increase the amount of infected fluid produced by people with HIV. Many people don't realize that they or their partner have these infections because the symptoms can be very mild.

Appearances
*It's impossible
to tell from
appearances
that someone
has HIV.*

Having sex during an infected woman's period could also be more risky because the partner would come into contact with her blood.

Anal sex, whether between a man and a woman or two men, is more risky than vaginal sex. This is because the lining of the rectum is thin and easily damaged. The risk is highest for the receptive (penetrated) partner. There is also a raised risk for the active (penetrating) partner because his penis may be exposed to blood from the damaged rectum.

HIV can be passed on during oral sex, but the risk is very low. It seems that the acid environment in the mouth and the natural antiseptics present in saliva have a protective effect. Sexual activities between two women (lesbian sex) also carry a very low risk of HIV infection.

Contact with infected blood

This happens in two main ways:

- ⬤ sharing needles when injecting drugs
- ⬤ through blood transfusions and other blood products.

Injecting drugs

People who inject themselves with street drugs (such as heroin) are at high risk of catching HIV. This is because drug users often share needles and syringes. A common and particularly risky habit is to draw blood into the syringe to flush out the last traces of the drug, and then force it back into the vein. Small amounts of blood are left in the equipment and get injected into the vein of the next person to use it. This is a very efficient way of spreading HIV (and other viruses like hepatitis B and C). Drug injecting has so far been responsible for about 1 in 12 of all reported HIV

Needles
In Berne, Switzerland, bins are provided for drug users to dispose of used needles. Preventing people from re-using discarded needles reduces the spread of HIV.

NUR SPRITZEN!

Nehmen Sie bitte Rücksicht auf unser Personal!

Strasseninspektorat der Stadt Bern

Piercing and tattoos

HIV and other viruses could be spread by body piercing or tattooing if the needles were infected. If you're thinking of having one of these done, choose a parlour that looks clean and well-run. Ask them beforehand what hygiene measures they take. All needles should be used just once and then disposed of.

Tattooing
A work of art – but make sure the needle is sterile!

infections in the UK and about a quarter of those in the USA. Some cities are now seeing AIDS epidemics among drug users.

Hospitals and clinics in the developed world use only new, sterile needles. However, lack of money means medical equipment elsewhere in the world is sometimes reused, with a potential risk of infection.

Blood transfusions

If someone with HIV donates blood, the person who receives it has about a 90 per cent chance of catching the virus. Thousands of people were infected in this way before 1985. Since then, developed countries have tested all donated blood for HIV antibodies, and people in high-risk groups (page 14) are asked not to give blood. There is a tiny risk (about 1 in 700,000) that the donated blood will come from someone who has HIV but has not yet developed antibodies. However, tests are now available which detect the virus itself (page 44), so blood supplies are getting even safer. Blood products like the clotting factors needed by haemophiliacs are now heat-treated to kill the virus, though whole blood cannot be treated in this way.

Poorer countries cannot always afford to test donated blood, so transfusions are still spreading HIV in some areas.

Mother-to-baby infection

Worldwide this is the second most common way that HIV is spread. Over half a million babies caught the virus from their mothers in 1999, 90 per cent of them living in Africa. Mother-to-baby infection can happen in three ways:

- before birth, when viruses from the mother's blood cross into the baby's
- during birth, when the baby is exposed to blood and vaginal fluids
- during breastfeeding.

Breastfeeding

Breastfeeding is normally the safest and healthiest way to feed a new baby. But a mother who is infected with HIV can pass on the infection this way.

Overall, the chance of an infected mother passing the virus to her baby is about 30 per cent. If she is newly infected or has advanced AIDS, the risk is higher. Treating the mother with the drug AZT during pregnancy cuts the risk to about 8 per cent.

'My brother is HIV-positive but we're just like normal brothers. We play football, play wrestling games, share drinks. I'm not scared. You can't catch AIDS like that.'
(Darren, 13)

How the virus doesn't spread

As we saw in chapter 2, HIV is a fragile virus that can't survive for long outside the body. This limits the ways in which it can spread. Researchers have done studies to see whether people who live in the same house as someone with HIV or AIDS ever get infected (obviously, sexual partners and needle sharers weren't included). No cases of infection were ever found. HIV does not spread through any day-to-day contact or ordinary activities, for example:

- *breathing the same air (HIV doesn't spread in droplets from coughs and sneezes)*
- *hugging or kissing (except possibly 'deep' tongue-in kissing)*
- *sharing knives and forks, telephones, toilets, bedding or any other items*
- *mosquitoes, fleas or bed-bugs.*

5 Avoiding infection
How to protect yourself

In chapter 4 we looked at the possible ways of catching the HIV virus. Luckily, there are effective ways to protect yourself against infection.

Safer sex
Waiting

The only way to be 100 per cent safe from sexually transmitted infections, including AIDS, is not to have sex! Deciding not to have sex for a while is called abstinence, and is perfectly normal even for adults. There are many reasons why abstinence can be the right choice:

- there is no risk of unplanned pregnancy or sexually transmitted infection
- not feeling ready for sex
- not being with the right person
- staying true to religious or other personal beliefs.

Deciding when to have sex is very personal, and anyone who respects you should also respect your decision.

Decisions
There is a lot to think about before bringing sex into a relationship.

If you want a physical relationship, there are lots of ways to enjoy each other's bodies without having full sex. Hugging, kissing and touching carry very little risk (as long as sperm and vaginal fluids don't get into contact with broken skin).

Faithful relationships

There is no risk if neither you nor your partner inject drugs and you are both virgins at the start of the relationship, i.e. you've never had sex with anyone else. The same applies to two people who know they are HIV-negative and have sex only with each other. Remember, though, that many people with HIV don't realize they are infected; if you've been sexually active before, the only way to be sure is to take a test. It is also true that some people will lie about their past or will secretly 'cheat' with other partners, however trustworthy they may seem to be.

'I just don't feel ready for sex yet, but there's a lot of pressure to lose your virginity. It's really hard to say "no".'
(Julie, 15)

Casual sex

The more sexual partners you have, the greater your risk of contact with someone who has HIV or another sexually transmitted infection (STI). Some people get into the habit of having sex with lots of different partners, perhaps people they have only just met. This lifestyle puts you at higher risk, especially if you don't always use condoms. People who sell sex – in exchange for money or drugs – have an even greater chance of infection.

Condoms and safer sex

If you do decide to have sex, it is very important to use a condom – at least until you are absolutely sure that your partner is free from HIV and other sexually transmitted infections. A condom is a latex (rubber) or polyurethane sheath that is placed over the penis before sex. Female condoms are also available: these are plastic sheets worn inside the vagina.

Studies have shown that latex and polyurethane condoms give very effective protection against HIV and other STIs that are spread through sexual fluids or blood. This is because they form a barrier which prevents contact with the partner's body fluids. In couples where one partner has HIV, condoms are 98-100 per cent effective at stopping the other from catching it. To get this level of protection, it is essential to use the condom *correctly* and to use it from *start to finish every time* you have vaginal, anal or oral sex. The Pill and other birth control methods do NOT give protection because they don't create a barrier (the diaphragm or cap forms a barrier at

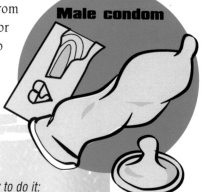

Male condom

How to use a condom

Condoms are only effective if used properly. Here's how to do it:

- Put the condom on the erect (hard) penis before any contact with the partner's genitals.

- Place the rolled up condom on the tip of the penis and pinch the end of the condom between your thumb and finger so that it does not fill with air. This leaves room for the sperm to flow into.

- Roll the condom down the penis right to the base, pulling the foreskin (hood) back gently to expose the penis tip.

- If the condom is not lubricated, moisten it with a water-based lubricant (you can buy these at the pharmacy). Don't use oil-based lubricants like Vaseline, baby oil or hand cream as these can weaken the condom.

- When withdrawing the penis after sex, hold the base of the condom to stop it falling off. Do this before the penis goes soft.

- Only use approved condom brands. Novelty condoms may not be effective. Condoms made from animal skin don't protect against STIs.

- Use an extra-strong brand of condom for anal sex.

- Don't use out-of-date condoms – check the expiry date on the packet.

- Use a new condom each time.

the top of the vagina but doesn't protect the lower part). For maximum protection against both STIs and pregnancy, doctors often recommend the 'double Dutch' method, i.e. using condoms and the Pill.

Condoms are less effective against diseases spread by skin-to-skin contact, for example herpes and genital warts. This is because the infectious skin can be outside the area covered by the condom.

Defenders
An AIDS awareness poster in Hanoi, Vietnam, conveys the idea that condoms are defenders in the battle against AIDS.

Changing behaviour

Are young people taking on board the safer sex message? The answer seems to be yes, and no. A survey in the USA has shown that sexually active high school students are more likely to use condoms than in the past, but over 40 per cent still aren't using them. This is worrying because under-25s are thought to account for at least half of all new HIV infections, and many of these will be teenagers.

Gay and bisexual men, who were the first to be hit by AIDS, did change their behaviour. Many started using condoms for anal sex, switching to safer sexual practices and cutting down on casual sex. As a result, infection rates fell. But some young gay men seem to be forgetting the lessons of the past. Because AIDS takes years to develop, they don't see its effects among their friends. There is a feeling that it only affects older men. One HIV worker, who has the virus himself, reports an 'amazing rise in unsafe sexual practices. It saddens me how men, especially young men, are not taking care of themselves. I find myself wanting to shake them.'

Drug injecting

People who inject drugs should always use their own needle and syringe. Many towns have needle exchange programmes where users can get sterile equipment and dispose of used items safely. In some areas needles and syringes can be bought from pharmacies or prescribed by doctors. Drug injecting can never be 'safe'; anyone with a drug problem should seek help.

Needle exchange

Used needles are exchanged for new ones in a programme in Vancouver, Canada.

Maria

Maria is 17 and HIV-positive. She caught the virus from Steve. 'I was totally in love with him, and we had sex soon after we met. We didn't use condoms because he said he didn't like them, and I was on the Pill anyway so I just thought, well, OK. I didn't really think there was any danger; you always think things like HIV happen to other people, not to you. When we'd been going out for about six months I found out that his ex-girlfriend was a drug user and that some of the people they hung around with had AIDS. I was quite scared and I went for a test, thinking it would put my mind at rest. When it came back positive it was like falling into a black hole. It still hits me every morning when I wake up. Maybe I'll come to terms with it one day, but I haven't yet. What makes it worse is how bitter I feel towards Steve. He must have known about the risk but he wouldn't even use a condom. I feel so stupid for trusting him. I don't know if I'll ever really trust anyone again.'

AZT

A pharmacist counts capsules of AZT, a drug that stops HIV from reproducing.

Protecting babies from infection

The drug AZT dramatically reduces the chances of an infected mother passing HIV to her baby, from 25-30 per cent down to about 8 per cent. Newer drugs may prove even more effective in the future. The mother is treated during pregnancy and the baby is given AZT for six weeks after birth. The baby is fed on formula rather than breast milk. Unfortunately, this treatment is not available in most developing countries, where most infected babies are born.

6 Testing and treatment
Drugs versus the virus

Testing for HIV

There are various tests available to find out whether someone is infected with the HIV virus. These are often called 'AIDS tests', but this is inaccurate because they test for the virus, not the disease. As we have seen, AIDS does not develop for several years or more after infection.

The most common type of test looks for antibodies (see page 19) to HIV in the blood. If these are found, it means that the person is infected. This is known as being HIV-positive. If no antibodies are found, the person is either free of the virus or has caught it but has not yet produced antibodies. Antibodies take anything between one and six months to develop, and this is called the window period. People who test negative but are still worried can be retested six months later to be sure that they are clear (providing they don't put themselves at risk again in the meantime).

It is also possible to test for HIV itself by looking for viral proteins or fragments of virus RNA (genetic material). Viral protein tests are now used by blood banks as a back-up to the antibody test, in case blood has been donated by an infected person in the window period.

Viral RNA tests enable doctors to estimate the number of viruses present in the blood. They can use this information

HIV testing

A multi-pipette is used to perform an enzyme-linked immunosorbent assay (ELISA) test for antibodies to the HIV virus.

to see how a patient's disease is progressing and how well their drugs are working.

How accurate are the tests?

The latest antibody tests are extremely accurate. However, all positive results are confirmed with a second test before the person is told that they have HIV.

Taking a test: advantages and disadvantages

Before effective treatments were available, many people felt that there was no point in being tested for HIV. They didn't want to learn bad news if there was nothing they could do about it. Nowadays there are several good reasons for people to get tested if they think they are at risk. If you know you have HIV:

'I was amazed when the test was positive because I felt fine. I still do.' (Tony)

⦿ starting drug treatment early can help you stay healthy for longer

⦿ you and your doctor can keep a close eye on your health and treat any problems straight away

How the antibody test works

Testing is done on a plastic plate containing a set of small wells. Each well is coated with proteins from the HIV virus. The blood to be tested is allowed to clot, leaving behind a clear fluid called serum. When the serum is put into the wells, any HIV antibodies it contains will recognize and stick on to the HIV proteins. Next the serum is washed out and replaced with detector antibodies which stick to HIV antibodies. Finally the wells are rinsed again and a preparation is added which changes colour when it meets an enzyme carried on the detector antibody. If the blood contained HIV antibodies, the colour will change. The whole procedure is often carried out automatically on machines that can test hundreds of samples at a time. Saliva and urine can also be tested for antibodies in this way.

- 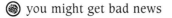 you can take up a healthy lifestyle: a balanced diet, keeping fit and generally taking good care of yourself can help you stay well
- you can protect other people by not putting them at risk
- if you are not infected, you can stop worrying unnecessarily.

There can also be disadvantages to being tested:

- you might get bad news
- people who are HIV-positive find it difficult to get insurance, mortgages, etc
- employers and insurance companies might want to check your medical records and might discriminate against you, even if your test was negative.

Healthy eating
People with HIV need to take good care of their bodies; a well-balanced diet can help.

Where can I get tested?

Before having a test, think about whether you want it to be anonymous. If in doubt, ask before you give any information.

Your family doctor (GP) can arrange a test for you. They will not tell your parents without your permission, even if you are under 16. However, the test and its result may be noted in your medical records. Anonymous testing is available from NHS sexual health clinics – these are also known as STD clinics and genito-urinary medicine or GUM clinics. You can find the number of your nearest clinic in the telephone book under STD or 'genito-urinary', or by phoning the switchboard of your local hospital.

Anonymous testing

Possible discrimination can be avoided if the test is done anonymously. In this case, no link is ever made between the name of the person being tested and their result. Instead, your test is given a code or number. When you come for the result you give the code and your result is found. The clinic doesn't even have to know your name or address, and no one can find out that you've had the test. Anonymous testing is available from hospital clinics in the UK and Health Department testing centres in the USA. Tests taken through your doctor will usually be noted down in your medical records.

Counselling

Everyone who has an HIV test should be offered counselling before and after the test. The counsellor will make sure that you understand what the test

Counselling
Getting tested can be traumatic, but you don't have to face it alone.

Adrian's testing dilemma

Adrian has found out that an ex-partner has developed AIDS, and he is worried. He is thinking about getting tested but isn't sure that he wants to. Could he cope with knowing that he was HIV-positive? Would his current partner leave him? What if his boss found out? He feels that a positive test would ruin his life. On the other hand, he knows that if he was infected he would stand a better chance of staying healthy by getting treatment early. And can he face years of uncertainty and worry that might not even be necessary? The stress of trying to weigh it all up is tearing him apart. He decides to phone an AIDS helpline. Perhaps talking it over with a counsellor will help him reach the right decision.

means and the advantages and disadvantages of going ahead. When giving the result, they offer support and information if the test is positive and advice on avoiding future risks if it is negative.

Treating HIV and AIDS

There is currently no cure for HIV. Once someone is infected it is impossible to completely remove the virus from their body. However, there are now drugs that can suppress it, enabling infected people to stay healthy for longer and dramatically improving the health of those who have already developed AIDS. In the UK, the death rate from AIDS fell by two-thirds between 1995 and 1999 (the new drugs were introduced in 1996). Some doctors now regard HIV/AIDS as a controllable long-term condition, rather than the always-fatal illness it once was. A few even think that we may soon be able to cure people of the virus altogether, providing that treatment is given early.

A drawer of drugs

People with HIV/AIDS need to take many different drugs each day. At a centre for AIDS patients, each person's drugs are kept in an individual drawer.

Most HIV and AIDS patients take a combination of three anti-retroviral drugs from the 15 or so that are available. This is called combination therapy or highly active anti-retroviral therapy (HAART). Single drugs are not as effective because the virus quickly becomes resistant to them – that is, it finds ways to reproduce that are not affected by the drug.

The drugs are called anti-retrovirals because they target specific points in the life-cycle of retroviruses, especially HIV. There are two classes available so far, one interfering with the viral enzyme called reverse transcriptase and one with another viral enzyme called protease. Enzymes are protein-based molecules that are essential for life; with these enzymes out of action, the virus cannot reproduce properly.

Monitoring disease progress

Once someone is diagnosed with HIV or AIDS, they should have tests every three to six months to see how the disease is progressing. One test measures the number of viruses circulating in the blood, known as the viral load. The other counts the number of CD4 cells (the immune system cells attacked by HIV). The more viruses and the fewer CD4 cells, the more active or advanced the disease. This information is used by doctors to decide when the person should start taking anti-retroviral drugs, and to assess how effective

The biological 'arms race'

Scientists all over the world are working on new ways to attack HIV. Perhaps one day they may find a cure. However, it is more likely that they will come up with ways of controlling the virus that are more effective or have fewer side effects than the treatments available now. Equally, the problem of resistance (see page 52) means that new drugs will be needed just to keep pace with the changes in the virus. This power struggle between scientists and virus has been likened to an 'arms race' between enemy countries, each trying to develop more powerful weapons than the other.

AIDS research

A scientist in protective clothing works on samples infected with HIV.

the treatment is. If it is successful, the viral load should drop so low that no viruses can be detected. But this doesn't mean that the virus has gone; it is still there, hiding in the lymph glands and nervous system.

When should treatment start?

Nowadays, people often start taking anti-retroviral drugs before they develop any symptoms. The decision on when to begin is made between the patient and their doctor. Early treatment could slow down the damage to the immune system and keep the person well for longer. On the other hand, side effects from the drugs could make their life difficult, and there is a risk that drug resistance could develop and limit their treatment choices in the future.

People who already have AIDS are treated straight away, and often experience a big improvement. They get fewer infections, put on weight and many can start leading a full life again. However, their damaged immune system cannot yet be rebuilt. HAART drugs can buy time but they are not a cure.

Treating infections and cancers

Treatments are available for some of the infections, cancers and other conditions that affect people with AIDS. For example, bacterial infections are treated with antibiotics and fungal infections with anti-fungal drugs. Some people take drugs to prevent common infections from developing, especially PCP pneumonia.

PCP pneumonia

A drug is inhaled to prevent PCP pneumonia, a dangerous infection in AIDS patients.

Problems with anti-retroviral treatment

Anti-retroviral drugs have dramatically improved the lives of many people with HIV and AIDS, but they are not without problems. The main one is drug resistance (see page 52). Often, a drug combination will keep the virus under control for a while but then become ineffective because resistance has developed. The patient then has to use another combination. Sometimes the virus becomes resistant to a whole series of drugs, and the patient runs out of treatments.

Other patients give up their drugs because of side effects. These vary from person to person but can be severe. They include anaemia (lack of iron in the blood, which causes tiredness and weakness), nausea (feeling sick), headaches and a condition called lipodystrophy, where extra body fat develops on the belly, shoulders and neck and fat is lost from the face, arms and legs. Because HAART has to be taken for life, even quite mild side effects can become a big problem over time.

Sticking to the schedule

To be effective, HAART drugs must be taken to a strict timetable. If doses are regularly missed, the virus has a chance to reproduce and develop resistance. The treatment will then become useless. The timetable can involve taking up to 25 pills a day, plus any other drugs the person needs.

Lucy

At the moment I take 28 pills a day. Every morning I feel like throwing up, and sometimes I wonder what I'm doing to my body and whether it's worth it. But the tests say the virus is under control, and I haven't had an infection for nine months. So I guess I'll keep taking them and just try to get on with life.

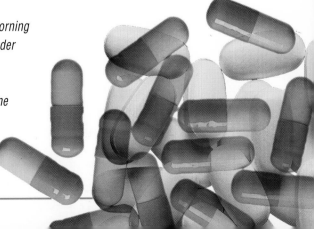

Mutations and resistance: the changing face of HIV

When HIV reproduces, it uses the enzyme called reverse transcriptase to make a genetic copy of itself inside the host cell. However, this process is not 100 per cent accurate. Mistakes are often made, so that the copy is not quite the same as the original. These mistakes are called mutations. Sometimes the mutation makes the copy useless, i.e. unable to produce working virus particles.

Occasionally a mutation arises that changes a part of the virus affected by a particular drug. The change does not stop the virus working, but it means that the drug can no longer lock on to its target. The mutated virus type is said to be resistant to the drug. It is now at an advantage and quickly spreads to infect more cells. Soon, the drug becomes ineffective and the patient must find another one. If they infect someone else, that person's infection will be resistant too.

To make things even more complicated, some HAART drugs can only be taken on a full stomach, others only on an empty stomach. For some people, keeping to this schedule every day, month after month, is too much to cope with.

Cost

Anti-retroviral drugs are expensive. A course of HAART can cost £4,000-14,000 ($6,000-21,000) per year. This is completely out of reach of most people in developing countries, who make up the majority of those affected by the virus. In 2001, drug manufacturers responded to public pressure by cutting prices in poorer regions, but cost remains a huge problem. In some developed countries people who don't have health insurance may find it difficult to pay.

AIDS vaccines: an impossible dream?

The best way of overcoming AIDS would be to develop a vaccine to stop people catching it in the first place. Many other viral diseases have been successfully tackled with vaccines, but with HIV the situation is more complicated for various reasons:

- the way the virus interacts with the immune system
- its rapid mutation rate and many different sub-types
- problems in finding enough people to test a vaccine (no one wants to expose themselves to the virus if the vaccine they've been given doesn't work)
- the enormous costs involved: drug companies don't think they could make a profit and fear huge demands for compensation if a vaccine went wrong.

Despite 15 years of intensive research, only a few potential vaccines have made it far enough to be tested on humans. There have been many setbacks, and some scientists believe that a safe, effective vaccine that covers a range of HIV sub-types may prove impossible to develop. Nevertheless, work is continuing, including some larger-scale human trials.

Vaccine research
Research into a vaccine to protect against AIDS, University of Cape Town Medical School, South Africa.

7 Living with HIV and AIDS
Good days and bad days

Prejudice and discrimination

Like any other life-threatening disease, AIDS and HIV infection are hard to come to terms with. However, those with HIV/AIDS often face the added difficulty of negative reactions from other people. Common reactions include fear, disgust, moral judgement (the idea that catching HIV involves doing something 'bad'), outright hostility and even violence. Unlike someone with, say, cancer, people with HIV/AIDS can sometimes

- lose their job
- be thrown out of the place where they live
- lose their partner
- be rejected by the people around them
- face verbal abuse and even physical violence or damage to their property.

'It would be easier if I had cancer. With cancer you get sympathy; with AIDS, you get disgust.' (Linda)

Prejudice and discrimination were especially bad in the early years of the epidemic, when most people were ignorant about the virus and how it could and could not spread. It was seen as something that only affected gays and drug users, not 'respectable' people. At the same time, people were afraid that even everyday contact with those infected could be dangerous. Unfortunately, these ignorant attitudes are still around today. What people affected by HIV really need is acceptance and support.

Many forms of discrimination are illegal, but this does not always stop them from happening. As we saw on page 46, a positive HIV test – or even just taking a test – can lead to problems with employment, insurance and relationships. For this reason, testing can be arranged anonymously, so that no one else can find out about it.

'If someone gets AIDS from a blood transfusion, the media talks about 'innocent' victims – as if people like me deserve AIDS just because we're gay.'
(David)

PHILADELPHIA

Philadelphia

In the 1993 film 'Philadelphia', Tom Hanks (left) plays the part of a lawyer who develops AIDS. His employers sack him and he takes them to court. His lawyer for the case (played by Denzel Washington) begins with some fears and prejudices about AIDS, but loses these as he gets to know his client.

Acceptance
*People with AIDS need love and
support, not judgement.*

Young people are affected too

In the early days of the AIDS epidemic, some HIV-positive children were banned from school in case they infected classmates. Others had to play alone because friends were forbidden from contact by anxious parents. Nowadays children and teens with HIV can usually stay in school, but most keep their condition secret for fear of bullying and rejection.

'People say stuff like "what an AIDS virus"; they use it as an insult about someone. I just keep quiet. If they knew, they would take me to pieces.'
(David, 12, who has HIV)

HIV also affects the lives of children and teenagers if a member of their family has the virus. They face a double anxiety: worrying about their relative's health and whether they will die, and worrying about what other people will think if they find out.

Lisa

Lisa was 13 when her dad became ill. He started off being tired all the time and then began to spend more and more days in bed. One day he developed a very high fever and was taken to hospital. 'I kept asking what was wrong with him,' remembers Lisa, 'but mum just said she didn't know.' Over the months he lost a lot of weight and became very weak. Finally, he told Lisa that he had AIDS. Lisa was told to say that her dad had cancer, because her parents were afraid that the family might be bullied. He died the following year. Soon after the funeral, one of Lisa's classmates found out that he had had AIDS. 'Suddenly a lot of people didn't want to know me. They were saying terrible things about dad and they wouldn't sit next to me because they said I must have AIDS too. I cried every night.' Lisa couldn't understand how people could be so ignorant and cruel. 'Only my two best friends stood by me. They were shocked at first but they accepted it.'

Living with HIV and AIDS

Knowing that you have the HIV virus means knowing that one day you will almost certainly get ill and eventually die from AIDS. People who already have AIDS go through months or years of suffering for which there is no cure. Many have lost friends and loved ones. People cope with these situations in different ways. Some become angry and bitter. Others find new meaning to their lives, perhaps through helping others, through spiritual beliefs, or just by concentrating on the things that are really important to them. For most, life with HIV/AIDS is a mixture of good days and bad days.

'I've lost some dear friends to AIDS. I'm almost the only one left, and at the moment my health is good. Sometimes I feel guilty about that. Why do I deserve to live, and not them?' (Gary)

'Living with HIV bonds you together and makes friendships very precious.' (Paul)

Since 1996, new drugs have made the future brighter – for those who can afford them and for whom they work.

People who thought their lives were almost over are now fit and healthy, at least for the time being. For them, living with HIV and AIDS now means rebuilding their lives. They face new challenges: who will give them a job? will they be able to find a loving relationship again? how long will the drugs keep working?

In the background, scientists are working on new drugs and vaccines that may one day bring HIV and AIDS under control. Sadly, for the majority of people affected – those who live in developing countries – help is still far off. AIDS has affected humanity more deeply than probably any other disease in history, and its impact is far from over.

World AIDS Day

Children march in Nairobi, Kenya, for World AIDS Day.

Glossary

anal sex — when the penis enters the anus, either of a woman or of another man.

anonymous — literally, of unknown name. Anonymous tests refer to a person by a code rather than by name.

antibodies — proteins made by the immune system to fight specific infections.

anti-retroviral drugs — drugs that work against retroviruses such as HIV.

anus — the opening of the digestive tract (bum hole or butt hole).

bisexual — attracted to or having sex with people of both sexes.

blood transfusion — when blood donated by one person is given to another.

CD4 cells — another name for T-helper cells (see page 61).

chromosomes — structures found in the cell nucleus, made up of long DNA molecules which carry thousands of genes.

condom — rubber or plastic sheath that fits over the penis to prevent pregnancy and STIs. Female condoms are rubber or plastic sheets worn inside the vagina. (Unlike caps or diaphragms, they cover the whole vagina.)

counselling — guidance from a trained person about a particular issue, such as HIV testing.

developed world — the rich, industrialized countries, such as Europe and North America.

developing world — poorer countries with less developed economies.

discrimination — treating someone unfavourably because, for example, they have HIV.

DNA — deoxyribonucleic acid, the molecule that carries the genetic code in nearly all living things.

electron microscope — a powerful microscope that uses electrons instead of light to form an image, giving very high magnifications.

enzymes — a class of protein-based molecules that are essential to many of the chemical reactions that take place within living things.

epidemic — an outbreak of disease affecting many people in a community at the same time.

faithful relationship — a relationship in which the partners have sex with each other and no one else.

gay — homosexual, i.e. attracted to people of the same sex.

genitals — the external sex organs.

heterosexual — attracted to or having sex with someone of the opposite sex.

HIV-positive — having antibodies to HIV, meaning that the person is infected with the virus.

homosexual — attracted to or having sex with someone of the same sex.

immune system — the system of specialist cells and chemical messengers that protects us from infections.

infectious — spread from one person to another; (of a person) capable of infecting other people.

microbes/ micro- organisms — microscopic life-forms, i.e. bacteria, viruses, fungi and microscopic animals.

mutations — small changes in the genetic code.

nervous system — the network of nerve cells, including the spinal cord and the brain.

opportunistic infection — illness caused by a normally harmless microorganism that gets past a damaged immune system.

parasites — animals that live on or inside humans or other animals.

pneumonia — a serious condition involving inflammation of the lungs; can be caused by various microbes.

prostitute — someone who has sex for money.

proteins — molecules made up of chains of chemicals called amino acids. They are present in all living things and have many different functions.

rectum — the end of the digestive tract, just inside the anus.

resistance — when a microorganism has undergone changes which stop a drug from working against it.

retrovirus — a family of viruses, including HIV, that have RNA as their genetic material.

RNA — ribonucleic acid. Closely related to DNA; it carries the genetic code in some viruses, including HIV.

sexually active — taking part in physical sexual relationships.

sterile — free from microorganisms (e.g. bacteria and viruses).

STI/STD — sexually transmitted infection or disease: an infection passed from one person to another during sexual contact.

symptoms — the physical effects produced by a disease, e.g. rash, pain, fever.

T-helper cells — one of the cell types that make up the immune system, and the type that is destroyed by HIV. Also called CD4 cells.

tissues — the collections of cells that make up the parts of the body, e.g. muscle tissue, skin tissue.

tuberculosis — serious disease affecting the lungs and sometimes other organs, caused by bacteria called *Mycobacterium tuberculosis*.

viral load — the number of viruses found in a given amount of blood.

wasting — severe loss of body weight.

white blood cells — blood cells, known as leucocytes, which function as part of the immune system.

Resources

Organizations

AVERT (AIDS Education and Research Trust)
4 Brighton Road, Horsham,
West Sussex RH13 5BA
Tel. 01403 210202

Produces user-friendly literature on AIDS and safer sex, including information for young people.

Children With AIDS Charity (CWAC)
Lion House, 3 Plough Yard,
London EC2A 3LP
Tel. 020 7247 9115

Helps children with AIDS and their families. Also produces publications and videos.

Terrence Higgins Trust
52-54 Gray's Inn Road, London WC1X 8JU
Tel. 020 7831 0330

Europe's largest HIV/AIDS charity. Provides support and information to people living with HIV/AIDS and information on risks and safer sex.

American Foundation for AIDS Research (AmFAR)
120 Wall Street, 13th Floor,
New York, NY 10005-3902
(212) 806-1600

Non-profit organization that supports AIDS research and education.

Helplines

National AIDS Helpline
0800 567 123
Free, confidential helpline, available 24 hours a day. Can give you the address of your nearest NHS STD clinic.

Lesbian and Gay Switchboard
020 7837 7324
Information and advice on sexuality and safer sex. Open 24 hours.

Terrence Higgins Trust Direct Helpline
0845 1221200

Index

Note

The photographs for the case studies were all posed by models.

CONTENTS

Some words are shown in bold, **like this**. You can find out what they mean by looking in the glossary.

A BORN GENIUS

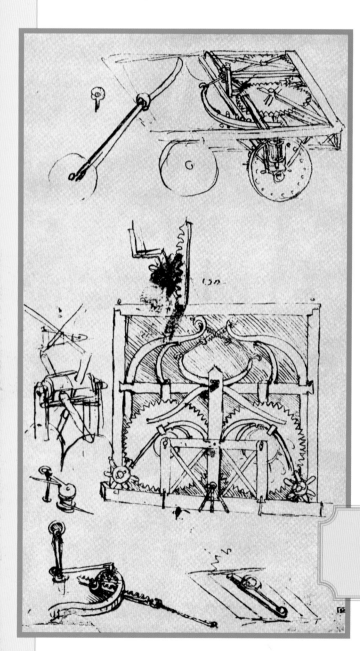

Leonardo da Vinci lived more than 500 years ago. He lived in Italy. He was a clever person and was interested in science, buildings, and machines. He was also interested in inventions and art. Leonardo wanted to know as much as he could about his favourite subjects.

He lived long before helicopters, cars, bicycles, and battle tanks. These were machines of the future. Leonardo thought of them all, hundreds of years before they were built.

This sketch shows a design for a self-propelled cart. Leonardo drew this around 1480.